health & nutrition

Developed by Macmillan Educational Company
Written by Julie Konieczko
Text illustrated by Eleanor Wasmuth
Cover illustrated by Patrick Girouard

Newbridge Educational Programs

TABLE OF CONTENTS

TABLE OF CONTENTS
Continued

Cut out the four pictures at the bottom of this page.
Look at what the child in each picture is wearing.
Then read the sentences that tell about each weather scene.

Name_____

Glue each picture in the box next to the weather scene it matches.

SUMMER

It is sunny and hot.

FALL

It is windy and cool.

WINTER

It is cold and snowy.

SPRING

It is raining.

DELIGHTFUL DEVILED EGGS

Ingredients: ten hard-boiled eggs (cooled)
¼ cup mayonnaise
2 teaspoons mustard
1 tablespoon chopped green onion

How to Make:

1. Peel the eggs. Save some of the shells to use in the cola experiment on this page.

2. Cut the eggs in half lengthwise. Rinse the knife occasionally to keep it from sticking.

3. Remove the yolks and mash them with a fork in a bowl.

4. Add the mayonnaise, mustard, and chopped green onion. Mix well.

5. Use a teaspoon to stuff the egg halves with the yolk mixture.

6. Serve the deviled eggs to the class for a healthy snack. (Deviled eggs are in the meat and meat alternates food group.)
(Makes 20 servings.)

SUGAR AND CAVITIES

You need: two white eggshells (saved from preparing the deviled-egg recipe on this page)
water
two empty, clean, clear glass jars
regular cola
toothbrush
toothpaste

Steps:

1. Explain to children that sugar hurts teeth. It can eat away at a tooth and make a hole, or *cavity,* in it. Tell children that brushing their teeth every day will help keep sugar from making cavities.

2. Then tell children that you are going to show them what sugar can do to teeth. Explain that eggshells are made of calcium, the same thing that teeth are made of.

3. Rinse the eggshells in water, and place one in each glass jar. Pour enough regular cola into one jar to cover the eggshell. Then pour enough water into the other jar to cover the eggshell. After a few minutes observe both eggshells. Tiny bubbles will form on the surface of the eggshell in the cola.

4. Explain to children that many soft drinks have a lot of sugar in them, but that water has no sugar.

5. Let the eggshells sit in the liquids overnight. The next day, remove the eggshells and compare them. The shell from the jar of cola will be stained brown and will have disintegrated slightly. The shell from the jar of water will not have been affected.

6. Using a toothbrush with a bit of toothpaste on it, gently brush a part of the stained eggshell. You will remove the stain. Tell children that by brushing their teeth, they will not only remove stains but also foods that eat away at teeth.

Ask children to sit in a circle in a large, open area of the room, and read them this story. As you tell the story, do the actions in parentheses and have children imitate your movements.

DEEP in the forest live two squirrels called Hale Hearty and Wilmus Weakblood. They are not at all alike. Hale Hearty is big and strong and has thick, shining fur. He is a happy squirrel. Wilmus Weakblood is small and always tired. His fur is thin and dull-looking. Wilmus is unhappy.

After a good night's sleep, Hale wakes up rested and ready for the new day. He stretches his arms and legs (*stretch broadly*) and fixes a good breakfast of eggs, toast, and milk. When Wilmus gets up, he is so tired that he can barely stretch (*stretch feebly*). Sometimes Wilmus eats leftover cake for breakfast, and sometimes he doesn't eat any breakfast at all.

After breakfast, Hale goes outside to play and exercise. He runs quickly (*run in place vigorously*) from here to there. Then Hale climbs up a tree (*make strong climbing motions*) and jumps far (*jump up high*) from branch to branch. Wilmus doesn't like to exercise. Most of the time he stays home and watches TV. When he does go out to exercise, he runs very slowly (*run in place weakly*). Wilmus is so tired after running that he has to take a long time to climb a tree (*make slow climbing motions*). He cannot jump very far at all (*make small jump*).

For lunch, Hale goes home and eats a sandwich, soup, and salad. Then he goes back outside and pulls weeds from his garden (*bend down and make strong pulling motions*). But not Wilmus. Wilmus eats lots and lots of gumdrops for lunch. He tries to pull weeds from his garden, but he just can't pull hard enough (*bend down and make weak pulling motions*). Then Wilmus goes back inside and watches more TV.

When it's time for supper, Hale cooks a healthy meal and has an apple for dessert. Then he cleans up, puts on his pajamas, and goes to bed on time so that he'll have plenty of energy for the next day (*put hands together and lean head on them, with eyes closed*). Instead of eating supper, Wilmus munches on pretzels and candy. He stays up late to watch a movie on TV. Then he goes to bed, but he tosses and turns all night (*close eyes and turn head from side to side while wiggling shoulders*). That's why, when Wilmus wakes up each morning, he is still so tired.

Discussion Questions:

1. How are Hale Hearty and Wilmus Weakblood different from each other?

2. What are some things Hale eats during the day? What are some things Wilmus eats?

3. How does Hale get exercise? Does Wilmus get exercise every day? Who gets more exercise?

4. Who gets more rest, Hale or Wilmus?

5. Who is happier, Hale or Wilmus? What could Wilmus do so that he would feel better?

Follow-up Activity:

Name some activities and ask children to show you how Hale would do them, and how Wilmus would do them. Some suggestions: carry a heavy suitcase; paddle a canoe; march in a parade; sweep the floor; swing at a baseball.

Name_____

Wilmus Weakblood wants to know how he can be strong and healthy like Hale Hearty. Look at the pictures below. Read the health rule in each box. Draw a circle around the picture in each box that shows what Wilmus needs to do to be healthy. In the empty box, draw a picture of healthy, strong Wilmus.

Use this activity at the beginning of the school year to introduce children to classroom safety rules.

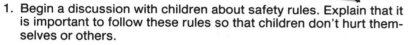

You need: badge cutout on this page
pencils
crayons
scissors
glue
5″ circles cut from colored
    construction paper
scraps of ribbon
masking tape

Steps:

1. Begin a discussion with children about safety rules. Explain that it is important to follow these rules so that children don't hurt themselves or others.

2. On the chalkboard, write a few basic classroom safety rules; for example:

    Put away toys and supplies when they are
      not being used.
    Keep objects out of your mouth.
    Always walk, don't run, in the halls and classroom.
    Do not throw anything at another person.
    When carrying scissors, hold them closed with hands
      around the point.

    Then ask children if they can think of any other rules that would help keep the classroom a safe place for everyone. Write their suggestions on the chalkboard and add others that the children may have overlooked.

3. Reproduce the safety detective badge cutout on this page for each child. Distribute the badges.

4. Have each child write his or her name on the line provided and then color the badge.

5. Ask each child to cut out his or her badge and glue it onto a colored construction paper circle.

6. Children then glue one or two short lengths of ribbon onto the backs of their badges, as shown.

7. Next attach a loop of masking tape, sticky-side out, to the back of each child's badge. The child then presses the taped side of the badge onto his or her clothing.

8. Encourage each child to be a "safety detective" and watch out for any unsafe situations in the classroom. Children should call anything they notice to your attention.

Variation:

Discuss traffic safety or playground safety rules with your class, and have children make and wear their badges to remind them of these rules.

Step 6

SAFETY
DETECTIVE

_____
child's name

Follow-up Activity:

After discussing classroom safety rules, make copies of the worksheet on page 10 for children to complete.

Look at the picture below.
Circle each unsafe thing you see.
Color the picture.
Then tell why you circled the things you did.

Name_____

Read the story below. Use the key to learn which word each picture stands for. Then cut out the four boxes on this page. Put the boxes in order. Write numbers from 1 to 4 in the circles on the boxes and glue them in order on a strip of paper.

Name _____

To stay ☺ , you must keep your 🖐🖐 clean.

If your 🖐🖐 are covered with ▓ and 😖😖 ,

you might get 😷 . Here is how to wash ▓ and

😖 😖 off your hands:

1. Wet your 🖐🖐 with 🚰 .

2. Rub your 🖐🖐 with 🧼 .

3. Rinse the 🧼 off your 🖐🖐 with 🚰 .

4. Use a 🧻 to dry your 🖐🖐 .

Remember to wash your 🖐🖐 before you eat. Having

clean 🖐🖐 will help keep you ☺ .

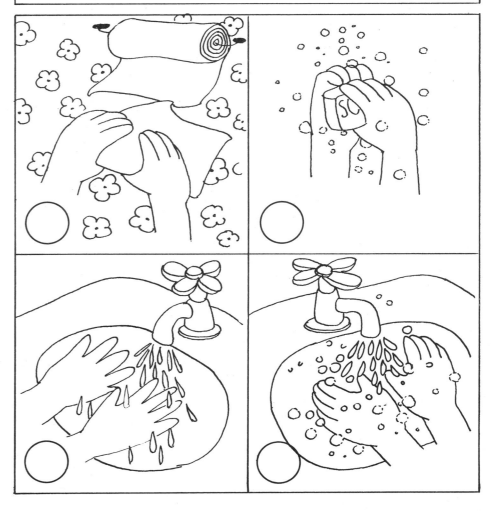

KEY

hands— 🖐🖐 healthy— ☺ germs— 😖😖 paper towel— 🧻

water— 🚰 soap— 🧼 sick— 😷 dirt— ▓

Read the story on this page to your class and then ask the discussion questions that follow.
To help children become aware of different types of physical impairments, do the activities described
on pages 13 and 14.

WHEN Helen Keller was born in 1880, she could do what any other baby could do. She could see her toys and hear her parents' voices. Helen was a happy little girl. Then one day, before she was two years old, Helen became very sick—so sick that she could not see or hear anything at all.

Helen got over her sickness, but she could never again see or hear. Sometimes Helen knocked things over and broke them because she couldn't see them. She could never go outside alone. Mr. and Mrs. Keller had to watch Helen all the time so that she would not hurt herself. They could not show or tell Helen what she needed to know. Helen couldn't play games or learn to read and write like other children.

When Helen was seven years old, her parents knew that they must do something to help her. One day Mr. Keller took Helen to visit Dr. Alexander Graham Bell, a famous inventor and teacher of the deaf. Dr. Bell told Mr. Keller that, even though Helen couldn't see or hear, she could learn by using her sense of touch. Dr. Bell helped Mr. Keller find a special teacher for Helen.

Soon after, Anne Sullivan became Helen's teacher and came to live with the Kellers. She taught Helen words for different objects by spelling out their names on Helen's hand and then having Helen touch the objects. The first word that Helen learned in this way was *water*. Again and again, Anne Sullivan spelled *W-A-T-E-R* on Helen's hand and then let water from a pump run over Helen's fingers. Finally, Helen understood that the name for this wet, cool substance was water.

Once Helen found out how to learn, she wanted to know everything. With Anne Sullivan's help, Helen learned to read. Because she could not use her eyes to read, Helen learned *braille,* a special alphabet of small, bumpy dots. Helen could feel these dots with her fingertips.

When she grew up, Helen learned to do many things that no one had ever thought a blind and deaf person could do. She went to college, wrote books, and traveled all over the world. Wherever she went, Helen Keller helped other blind and deaf people learn.

Discussion Questions:

1. How did Helen Keller become blind and deaf?

2. Who became Helen's teacher?

3. How did Anne Sullivan teach Helen the names of things?

4. What was the first word Helen learned?

5. Since she couldn't use her eyes, with what did Helen read?

6. What were some of the things Helen Keller did when she was grown up?

Listening Activity / Blindfold Activity

Use the activities on this page and page 14 to make children aware of how people's physical abilities vary. Stress the fact that people with physical impairments are just like everyone else—they simply do some things differently.

WHAT IF YOU COULDN'T HEAR?

You need: tape recording of a children's story
tape recorder

Steps:

1. In advance, record on tape a children's story with which most of your students are not familiar.

2. At story time, start the tape at normal volume and have the children listen.

3. As the tape is playing, reduce the volume little by little so that it becomes hard or impossible for the children to hear.

4. When children begin to complain that they cannot hear what is happening in the story, stop the tape. Ask the children how they felt when they could no longer hear the story.

5. Begin a discussion about hearing problems. Explain that some people cannot hear well and some cannot hear at all. Tell the class that some people with hearing problems wear hearing aids, which make it easier to hear. Others can understand what people are saying by watching (or "reading") their lips. Deaf people also use sign language, a special language that uses finger and hand motions to stand for letters and words.

6. At the end of the discussion, let children listen to the entire story at normal volume.

WHAT IF YOU COULDN'T SEE?

You need: newspapers
plastic measuring cup
1½ cups sand
blindfold
large paper cup

Steps:

1. Explain to children that blind people must use their other senses to do some things that most people do with the help of their eyes.

2. Spread newspapers on a table.

3. Fill the measuring cup with sand.

4. Blindfold one child and lead him or her to the table. Hand the blindfolded child the paper cup and the container of sand.

5. Explain to the child that he or she must pour the sand from the container into the paper cup, trying not to spill any of the sand.

6. Help the child place the tip of one index finger slightly inside the rim of the paper cup. Let the child begin pouring the sand into the cup, stopping when he or she can feel the sand with the tip of his or her finger.

7. Remove the blindfold and let the child see how well he or she did. Then have the child do the activity without the blindfold. Let each child try this activity. Then discuss with the entire class how they felt when they were unable to see what they were doing.

Use the activities on this page and page 13 to make children aware of how people's physical abilities vary. Stress the fact that people with physical impairments are just like everyone else—they simply do some things differently.

ARM SLING

You need: a piece of cloth large enough
to use as a sling
beach ball
pencil
paper

Steps:

1. Discuss with your class the concept of physical impairments. Explain that some people have *permanent* impairments that they will have all their lives. Others have *temporary* impairments, like a broken arm, which will heal in a few weeks.

2. Choose one child from the class. With a piece of cloth, make a sling to hold the arm the child uses when writing.

3. Gently toss a beach ball to the child and have the child try to catch it without using the arm in the sling.

4. Next ask the child to use a pencil and paper to try to write his or her name with the free hand.

5. Let each child do these tasks with one arm in a sling. Then ask children to describe how they felt when they could use only one arm. Ask children to offer suggestions about how they could help a friend who has broken his or her arm.

CRUTCHES

You need: set of adjustable crutches (which may be
borrowed from the school health department)

Steps:

1. Explain to children that some people can use only one of their legs. They may have to use crutches to help them walk.

2. Choose one child to try using crutches. Adjust the crutches so that they fit under the child's arms. Explain that to use the crutches properly you must lean your weight on the handholds of the crutches, <u>not</u> on the tops.

3. Have the child hold one foot off the floor and try to walk across the room, placing the bottoms of the crutches several inches ahead and then pulling the body forward until upright and stable.

4. Let each child try using the crutches. Then ask children how they felt when they had to use the crutches to walk. Have children name some activities that would be hard to do on crutches—running, going up or down stairs, carrying books, opening doors. Have children suggest how they could help a friend who had to use crutches.

Let children play this game to help reinforce good tooth care.

You need: game board on page 16
glue
9″ × 12″ oaktag
small objects to be used as playing pieces
(buttons, dried beans, paper clips)
die

Optional: clear plastic adhesive

Steps:

1. Reproduce the game board on page 16.

2. Mount it on oaktag. For durability, laminate or cover the game board with clear plastic adhesive.

3. Two to four children may play this game. Have each child select a playing piece and place it on the space marked *Start* on the game board.

4. Let the youngest child begin. He or she rolls the die and moves his or her playing piece that number of spaces along the trail on the game board. If the player's piece lands on a blank space, the player does nothing. If the space shows a picture of something that helps keep teeth healthy (toothbrush, toothpaste, apple, milk), the player rolls the die again and takes another turn. If the space shows something unhealthy for teeth (candy cane, cake, chocolate), the player must move his or her playing piece backward to the nearest blank space.

5. The game continues clockwise, each child rolling the die and moving his or her piece along the trail. The first player to reach the healthy tooth calls out "Good tooth checkup!" and becomes the winner.

Variation:

To play a more challenging version of this game, let older children use the food cards included with this unit. Prepare the food cards according to the directions on page 64. Then remove four cards from each of the five food groups and set them aside. Shuffle the remaining 30 cards and place them facedown in a pile next to the game board. In turn, each player draws the top card from the pile. If it shows a food from one of the basic four food groups, the player rolls the die and moves along the trail, following the rules of the simpler version given on this page. If the player draws a card showing a snack food, he or she loses the turn and does not roll the die. The first player to reach the healthy tooth calls out "Good tooth checkup!" and wins the game.

GOOD TOOTH CHECKUP
Game Board

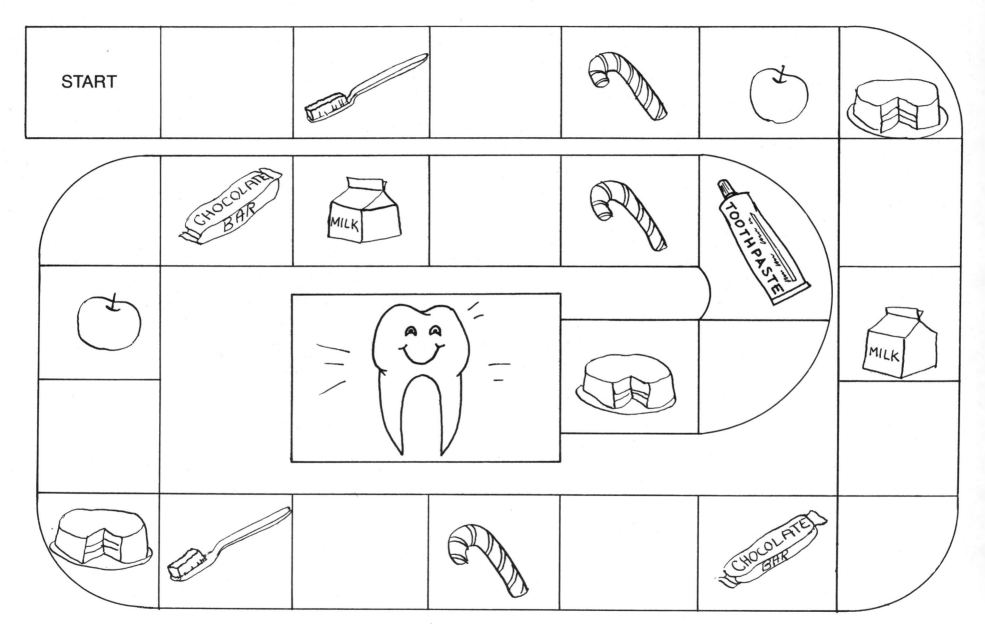

Use this activity to demonstrate to your class that proper storage keeps food from spoiling quickly.

You need: two slices of bread
two cups of milk
two small plastic sandwich bags
two clear glass jars with lids
masking tape
marker
worksheet on page 18
pencils

refrigerated October 8

not refrigerated October 8

Steps:

1. Explain to children that food will spoil and can make us sick if it is not stored properly. Food should be stored covered to keep germs off. Some foods need to be refrigerated as well.

2. Let children look at and smell the bread and milk. Then place each slice of bread in a plastic sandwich bag and close the bags. Next pour one cup of milk into each clear glass jar and put on the lids.

3. Attach a strip of masking tape to each bag and jar. With a marker, label one bag and one jar *refrigerated* and write the date on the strips. Label the other bag and jar *not refrigerated* and write the date on the strips.

4. Place the foods labeled *refrigerated* in the school refrigerator. (Be sure to notify the kitchen staff of your experiment.)

5. Set the foods labeled *not refrigerated* on a shelf in the classroom.

6. Next make a copy of the worksheet on page 18 for each child. Ask children to write down their descriptions of the foods in the spaces provided under the heading *Day 1*.

7. Observe the foods every three days over a nine-day period. Allow children to open the bags and jars and smell the foods. Have children make notes on their worksheets each time they examine the foods.

8. As mold and other signs of spoilage appear, discuss them with the children. Discuss the fact that the refrigerated foods do not spoil as quickly as the others. Explain that the cooler temperature inside the refrigerator helps keep mold from growing.

Name _____

Each day, after you look at the foods that are refrigerated and not refrigerated, write down what you see in the boxes below.

	Day 1	Day 3	Day 6	Day 9
Bread refrigerated				
not refrigerated				
Milk refrigerated				
not refrigerated				

Name _____

With your teacher, read and talk about the facts on this page.

1. Food goes into your body when you put it into your *mouth.*

2. After you chew and swallow, the food travels through your *esophagus,* a long tube.

3. From the esophagus, the food goes into your *stomach.* There it is broken up into very tiny pieces.

4. Next, the food leaves your stomach and goes into your *intestines.* Nutrients from the food can now travel to other parts of your body through your blood.

5. The food your body cannot use leaves it when you go to the bathroom.

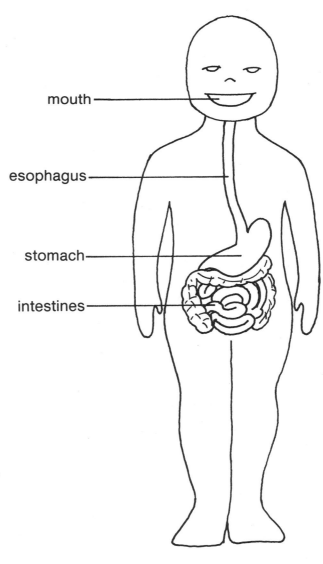

mouth

esophagus

stomach

intestines

Look at the four pictures of body parts below.
On the line next to each body part, write a number from 1 to 4 to
show the order in which food goes through a body.
Use your fact sheet for extra help.
Then cut out the pictures and paste them in order on a long
strip of paper.

Name_____

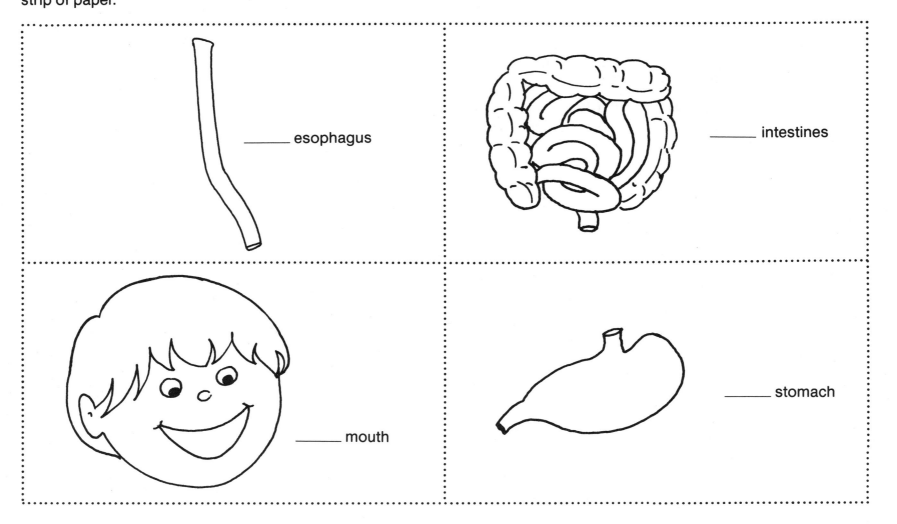

_____ esophagus

_____ intestines

_____ mouth

_____ stomach

ELWOOD'S PATH TO GOOD HEALTH
Maze Worksheet

Name_____

Help Elwood follow the path to reach good health. Draw a path from Elwood to the center of the maze. Do not cross any lines. Follow the pictures that show people, things, or activities that will help keep Elwood healthy. Stay away from pictures of things that are not healthy.

GOOD HEALTH

TOOTHPASTE

SOAP

SODA

Read the poem below. Using the underlined words in the poem, write your own recipe for growth.

Rules for Growth

To be healthy and to grow,
There are rules I need to know.

I must <u>sleep</u> each night for rest,
In order to look and feel my best.

I must <u>exercise</u> hard each day,
To help me grow in every way.

I'll <u>eat good food</u> to make me strong,
And give me energy all day long.

<u>Healthy habits</u> I will follow,
So that I'll feel well tomorrow.

These four rules I must know,
To stay healthy and to grow.

MY RECIPE FOR GROWTH

from the kitchen of_____
your name

_____

_____

_____

_____

THE ACTIVE PLAYGROUND
Worksheet

Everyone is having fun at the playground.
Draw circles around the children who are exercising.
Then answer the question at the bottom of the page.

Name_____

How many children in this picture are getting exercise?_____

Name_____

The animal athletes on this page are getting exercise, but they are all mixed up!
Color the pictures in each row.
Cut them apart along the dotted lines, one row at a time.
On another piece of paper, paste the pictures in rows so that each
animal is doing the exercise in the right order.

EXCELLENT EXERCISE
Art and Writing Activity / Game

Use these activities to help make children aware of the different ways in which they can get exercise.

WEEKLY EXERCISE JOURNAL

You need: 12″ × 18″ white construction paper
stapler
crayons

Steps:

1. Explain to children that they will be making exercise journals for one week to keep track of the exercise they get.

2. Give each child three pieces of 12″ × 18″ white construction paper. Have each child fold the papers in half to make a 12″ × 9″ booklet.

3. Staple each child's booklet together along the fold.

4. Next write *My Exercise Journal* on the chalkboard and have children copy the title onto the covers of their booklets. Children can then complete their covers by writing their names and drawing pictures of children getting exercise.

5. At the top of each of the next five pages in the booklet, each child will write the names of the days of the school week, from Monday through Friday.

6. Each day during the week, on the appropriate page, allow children time to draw pictures of any kind of exercise they did on that day. Children may write or dictate the names of the activities.

7. At the end of the week, discuss the different kinds of exercise the children included in their booklets. If desired, make a list of the exercises on the chalkboard and make a survey of how many children took part in the different types of exercise. Children may take their booklets home to keep as a record.

SIMON SAYS EXERCISE!

Steps:

1. Have children stand in an open area of the classroom or playground, leaving enough space between themselves to move freely.

2. Assign one child to be Simon. He or she stands in front of the other children, facing them.

3. Simon will call out commands for different types of exercise that the other players must pantomime or do; for example: "Simon says swim!" "Simon says dance!" "Simon says hop on one foot!" "Simon says jump rope!"

4. The other children must follow Simon's instructions only if the words "Simon says" come before the instructions.

5. If a child carries out the instructions when "Simon says" is not spoken, he or she must drop out of the game.

6. When only one player is left, he or she wins the game.

Follow-up Activity:

Play a game of charades after discussing the different types of exercise included in the children's booklets. Let individual children act out an activity in their booklets and have the other children try to guess what the activity is.

EXERCISE TRAIL
Large Motor Activity

Children will have fun moving along this exercise trail as they build their large motor skills.

You need: dark marker
9″ × 12″ oaktag
8″ soft rubber ball
masking tape
two shoe boxes
golf balls (one for each team member)
large spoons (one for each team member)
two large bowls
ten aluminum pie pans or 9″ paper plates
old pillowcase
stopwatch or watch with a second hand

Steps:

1. Set up a circular or linear exercise trail in a grassy play area. Establish a starting line, finish line, and five activity bases that are 10′ apart.

2. Using a dark marker, label separate sheets of oaktag *start, finish,* and *base 1* through *base 5*. Place the labels in position at the appropriate locations.

3. Set up the following activities for the five bases: base 1—ball toss, base 2—high jump and crawl, base 3—golf ball balance, base 4—pie pan tiptoe, and base 5—pillowcase hop. At base 1, place the 8″ soft rubber ball. At base 2, stack the shoe boxes with the long sides horizontal and tape together to create a hurdle. Put the golf balls and spoons in a bowl and place the bowl at base 3. At base 4, place an empty bowl. Then tape together the ten aluminum pie pans or paper plates side by side to form a chain. Put one end at base 4 and the other end pointing toward base 5. Then place the pillowcase at base 5.

4. Once you have set up the trail, show the children what they must do at each base and have a few children run through the trail as a demonstration. Then divide the class into equal teams of four or five children each. Tell them that you will time each team as they run through the trail. The team that gets through the trail with the

fastest time is the winner. Every time a player finishes the pie pan tiptoe at base 4, the next team member can leave the starting line.

5. To play, have one team line up behind the starting line. The first player runs to base 1, picks up the ball, and tosses it into the air and catches it five times. Any child who drops the ball must begin all over again. Once the activity is completed, the child skips to base 2. (If the child fails three times, he or she moves on to base 2.)

6. At base 2 the child jumps over the shoe box hurdle and crawls on hands and knees to base 3.

7. At base 3 the child places a golf ball in the bowl of a spoon and moves as quickly as possible to base 4. Any child who drops the ball must pick it up, put it back in the spoon, and continue to base 4.

8. At base 4 the child puts the ball and spoon in the bowl there, tiptoes on the chain of pie pans or plates (one foot on each pan or plate), and then runs to base 5.

9. At base 5, the child puts both feet into the pillowcase and, holding it up with his or her hands, jumps to the finish line and then back to base 5. He or she then removes the pillowcase, races to the finish, and sits down behind the other team members.

SHAPE UP WITH BRENDA BEAR
Worksheet

Cut out the sentences in the boxes at the bottom of the page.
Read each sentence and paste it under the picture it describes.
Then do the exercises that Brenda Bear is doing.

Name_____

1.	2.	3.

4.	5.	6.

Brenda Bear bends to the left.	Brenda Bear runs in place.	Brenda Bear bends to the right.
Brenda Bear reaches up to the sky.	Brenda Bear jumps rope.	Brenda Bear touches her toes.

Find ten words in the word puzzle that tell how you can get lots of exercise. The words are listed in the Word Bank. They may be written from top to bottom or from left to right. Some words may share some letters. One word has been circled for you.

Name

Word Bank	
hop	swing
skip	run
jump	hike
swim	climb
skate	dance

```
h r u n b h z d s
i c l x v o q a k
k z s k i p r n a
e s w f m k o c t
s w i n g u q e e
j u m p c l i m b
```

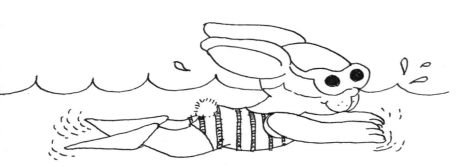

SILLY GYMNASTICS
Movement Activity

Use the ideas on this page to help children become aware of different parts of their bodies, and to reinforce the fact that exercise can be fun.

Steps:

1. Pair the children off as partners. Then tell the class that each twosome is responsible for inventing a special silly exercise—an exercise that no one has ever seen before. The silly exercises should be ones that each child can do alone.

2. Give the partners time to work together to discuss their plans. Lead them in their thinking with suggestions such as the following:

   ear-to-shoulder bends
   elbow claps
   finger wiggles
   knee lifts
   nose circles

3. Choose one pair to demonstrate their exercise to the class; then have the entire class join in and perform that exercise.

4. Have the next pair give a demonstration of their exercise, and then let the whole class join in. Continue in this manner until the class has performed every exercise.

Variations:

1. Have the class perform their silly exercises to music, each pair exercising simultaneously. Every time the music stops (stop the tape or lift the arm of the record player), the entire class freezes in position, mid-exercise.

2. Divide the classes into four teams. Each team must develop a series of silly exercises for a specific part of the body (a different exercise for each member of the team). The first team is assigned the arms; the second, the legs; the third, the waist; the fourth, the shoulders. After the members of the teams have demonstrated their invented exercises, the class votes on the silliest exercise for each part of the body.

3. Have the class form a single line. Play a tape or record that has a variety of tempos. The child at the head of the line leads the rest of the class through the room in a roundabout path while performing his or her silly exercise; the class follows along, imitating that exercise. Whenever you call out "Change leaders," the leader moves to the end of the line. As the new leader performs his or her silly exercise, the rest of the class follows along doing the new exercise.

With your teacher, read and prepare the recipe on this page.
(Makes about 15 half-cup servings.)

Name_____

1. Wash ____ .

2. Wash ____ ____ and ____ . Be sure the ____ have no ____ in them.

3. Peel and slice ____ ____ .

4. Separate ____ .

5. Cut ____ ____ into small pieces.

6. Put ____ ____ ____ plain yogurt and ____ honey in a ____ .

7. Stir in the ____ , ____ ____ , and ____ ____ .

8. Eat and enjoy!

KEY	
hands—	
apple—	
grapes—	
seed—	
banana—	
bowl—	
cup—	
half-cup—	

Discuss with children that the cooking process often changes the appearance and texture of foods.
Cooking makes some foods harder and other foods softer. It may also change the color of foods.
For the following experiments you may want to prepare enough foods so that each child can taste them in
their different forms. Raw eggs, of course, should not be tasted.

EGGS HARDEN

You need: three eggs
small saucepan
water
hot plate
spoon
marker or crayon
two paper plates
plastic knife
paper towels
small bowl
masking tape
margarine

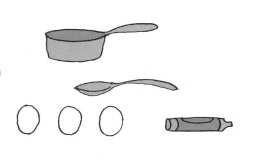

Steps:

1. Place one of the eggs in the saucepan and cover with cool water. Boil for 10 to 12 minutes. Remove from heat and drain. Remove the egg's shell. Label one of the plates boiled and put the egg on it. Slice the egg in half. Wipe the pan dry.

2. Crack one of the eggs into the bowl. Put a strip of masking tape on the bowl and label it *raw*.

3. Melt the margarine in the saucepan. Crack the third egg into the pan and stir over the heat until done. Label the second plate *scrambled* and put the egg on it.

4. Compare the three eggs. Discuss the parts of the egg and how they differ. Discuss the different textures of the eggs. Have the children think of other ways that eggs can be cooked and write them on the chalkboard.

CARROTS SOFTEN

You need: two or three carrots
knife
cutting board
saucepan
water
hot plate
marker or crayon
two paper plates
fork

Steps:

1. Wash and peel the carrots and cut them into strips.

2. Put half the carrot strips in the saucepan and cover them with water. Boil them for 10 minutes or until soft; drain. Label one of the plates *cooked* and put the cooked carrot strips on it.

3. Put the other half of the carrots on the other plate and label that plate *raw.*

4. Have the children compare the two plates of carrots, using the fork to mash part of the cooked carrots. Discuss how they differ.

5. Have the children think of other foods that soften when they are cooked and write them on the chalkboard.

BREAD DARKENS

You need: two or three slices of bread
two paper plates
toaster

Steps:

1. Put one slice of bread on one of the plates.

2. Toast one or two slices of bread in the toaster and put them on the other plate.

3. Discuss the differences in color and texture.

4. Have the children think of other foods that become dark when they are cooked and write them on the chalkboard.

COLD CHANGES FOOD
Edible Experiments

Here are some simple recipes that will demonstrate the effect of cold on certain foods. Have extra amounts of the major ingredients on hand and have the children taste and examine them before the recipes are prepared. Have the children describe the flavors and textures. Ask them whether they are solid or liquid. Then let the children help you make the recipes. As the children enjoy these treats at snack time, ask them to describe how the flavors, textures, and forms of the ingredients have changed.

FROZEN BANANA STICKS

Ingredients: 2 tablespoons honey
½ teaspoon vanilla
1 tablespoon milk
three bananas
six ice-cream sticks
1 cup flaked coconut

How to Make:

1. Measure the honey, vanilla, and milk into a mixing bowl. Mix until very smooth.

2. Peel the three bananas. Cut each banana in half at the middle. Insert an ice-cream stick into the cut end of each banana half.

3. Gently turn each banana half in the honey mixture until the banana is completely coated.

4. Sprinkle the bananas with flaked coconut.

5. Place the bananas on a waxed-paper-covered plate and freeze about three hours. (Makes six sticks.)

YOGURT POPS

Ingredients: 1 cup plain yogurt
½ cup grape juice or
orange juice
½ teaspoon vanilla
14 ice-cream sticks

How to Make:

1. Mix the yogurt, juice, and vanilla in a mixing bowl. Stir until the mixture is smooth.

2. Pour into a sectioned ice-cube tray.

3. Freeze 45 minutes or until the mixture is very thick but not frozen. Insert an ice-cream stick into the mixture in each compartment. Return to the freezer until frozen (about two hours). (Makes 14 yogurt pops.)

Variation:

Here's a delicious way to show children how powdered gelatin will dissolve when stirred into hot water and how, when refrigerated, that mixture will gel to various degrees. Simply prepare a 3-oz. package of fruit-flavored gelatin as directed, except substitute ¾ cup fruit juice for the cold water. Pour into small (3-oz.) paper cups, filling each cup half-full. Refrigerate until the mixture is thickened but not set. Insert an ice-cream stick or small plastic spoon into the mixture in each cup. Refrigerate until firm (about three hours). To eat, have children peel away the paper cups. (Makes about eight pops.)

You need: food checklist on page 34
pencils
napkins (one for each child)
three different types of food for
children to taste (see list
on this page)
cutting board
knife
three paper plates

Suggested Foods for Tasting

avocado	grapefruit	pear
cheddar cheese	mango	pickles
dates	mushrooms	pineapple

Steps:

1. Have children wash their hands before beginning this activity.

2. Make a copy of the food checklist on page 34 for each child. Then give each child a checklist, a pencil, and a napkin.

3. Explain to the class that there are many kinds of food to eat, and that different foods contain different nutrients that our bodies need. Tell children that it is important to eat several different kinds of food each day so that our bodies get all the nutrients they need. Then tell children that they will be tasting some interesting foods.

4. Discuss each of the foods you have selected for the children to taste. Pass the foods one at a time around the class, letting each child examine them. For each food, ask the following questions: What does it feel like? Is it smooth or rough? What color is it? What does it smell like? Can you hear anything when you shake it?

5. Wash the foods if necessary. Use a cutting board and a knife to cut each of the foods into bite-sized pieces (if appropriate) and place each food on a separate paper plate. Pass one plate around the class, letting each child take a piece of food. Ask the following questions: What color is the inside? How is it different from the outside? What does it feel like? How does it taste?

6. Write the name of the food on the chalkboard and have children copy it in the first numbered box on the checklist. Then ask children to make **X**'s in the column under the first numbered box next to the words that describe the food's texture, color, and taste.

7. Then pass around the second plate of food and have children taste it. Write the food's name on the board and ask children to fill in the name in the second numbered box and mark **X**'s in the appropriate boxes in the column under it. Then do the same with the third plate of food, and have children complete the third column on their checklists.

Variation:

With younger classes, have children simply taste and compare different foods without filling in the checklists.

TASTING PARTY
Checklist

Name_____

		1.	2.	3.
Texture	soft			
	crunchy			
Color	yellow			
	orange			
	red			
	brown			
	purple			
	green			
	white			
Taste	sweet			
	sour			
	salty			
	bitter			

Read the clues below and fill in the puzzle.
Use the Word Bank for extra help.

Name_____

Word Bank

cheese	fish
tomato	ham
oranges	eggs
bread	milk

ACROSS

1. This food is red and grows on a plant.

4. This food comes from pigs.

6. Milk is used to make this food.

8. These live in lakes and oceans.

DOWN

2. This food comes from cows.

3. These fruits grow on trees.

5. Flour is used to make this food.

7. Hens lay these.

THE MILK AND MILK PRODUCTS GROUP
Easy Recipes

Use the recipes on this page at snack time. Let children work in small groups measuring, pouring, and mixing with your supervision.

VITAMIN C EGGNOG

Ingredients: 6-oz. can frozen orange-juice
concentrate
2 cups milk
2 cups eggnog

How to Make:

1. Let the orange juice thaw in a mixing bowl.

2. Add the milk to the thawed juice. Beat until well blended. If desired, use a blender.

3. Stir in the eggnog. (Makes about eight ½-cup servings.)

ORANGE BUTTERMILK FROTH

Ingredients: 2 cups buttermilk
1 cup orange juice
1 scoop vanilla ice cream
2 tablespoons brown sugar

How to Make:

1. Pour the buttermilk and orange juice into a blender container.

2. Add the ice cream and sprinkle in the brown sugar.

3. Mix in blender until very smooth, about 10 seconds. (Makes about seven ½-cup servings.)

ZIPPY MILKS

Ingredients: milk (about 1 cup for each child)
honey, orange juice, or grape juice

How to Make:

1. Fill each child's cup or glass half-full with milk.

2. Have each child measure 1 tablespoon of honey or juice into his or her cup or glass and stir well.

3. Each child then adds more milk and stirs the mixture gently. Sip and enjoy!

EASY CHEESY SPREAD

Ingredients: small-curd cottage cheese (about ¼ cup
for each child)
chopped apples, pineapple chunks, raisins,
and chopped walnuts
bread or crackers

How to Make:

1. Let each child spoon a small amount of cottage cheese into a cup.

2. Place chopped apples, pineapple chunks, raisins, and chopped walnuts into separate bowls.

3. Have each child choose one fruit or nut ingredient and stir a table-spoon of that ingredient into the cottage cheese.

4. Children may then spread their cottage cheese mixtures onto bread or crackers.

Let children help make these recipes to highlight the fruits and vegetables food group.

PUPPY DOG FRUIT SCULPTURE

Ingredients: one or two lettuce leaves
one canned pear half
one canned prune
one raisin
one strawberry half
two canned mandarin orange sections

How to Make:

1. Children will love preparing and eating this tasty fruit salad. Wash the lettuce leaves, pat dry with a paper towel, and place on a small paper plate.

2. Place the canned fruits on a paper towel to drain.

3. Place the pear half cut-side down on the lettuce. With scissors, cut the prune in half lengthwise and remove the pit. Place one of the prune halves at the large end of the pear half to form the puppy dog's ear, as shown. (You can eat the other prune half.)

4. Make a tiny hole for the dog's eye and place the raisin in it. Place the strawberry half at the tip of the narrow end of the pear. This is the dog's nose. Set the mandarin orange sections along the rounded end of the pear half to make the collar.

GARDEN POTATO SALAD

Ingredients: water
six medium-sized potatoes, washed and peeled
one small onion, finely chopped
1/4 cup bottled Italian salad dressing
1/2 teaspoon salt
pinch of pepper
1/2 cup mayonnaise
one stalk celery, chopped (leaves included)
1/2 cup thinly sliced radishes
1/2 cup shredded carrots

How to Make:

1. Pour about three inches of water in a large saucepan. Add the potatoes and bring to a boil. Reduce the heat, cover, and cook about 30 minutes or until the potatoes are tender. Drain the potatoes and let cool.

2. Cut the potatoes into bite-sized chunks. Place in a mixing bowl.

3. Stir in the onion, salad dressing, salt, and pepper. Cover and refrigerate until chilled, at least two hours.

4. Just before serving, add the mayonnaise, celery, radishes, and carrots. Toss gently until well mixed. (Makes about 10 to 12 servings.)

Have your class help you prepare and enjoy these tasty treats.

Ingredients: 1 egg
1 cup flour
3/4 cup milk
2 tablespoons vegetable oil
1 tablespoon sugar
3 teaspoons baking powder
1/2 teaspoon salt
powdered sugar or maple syrup

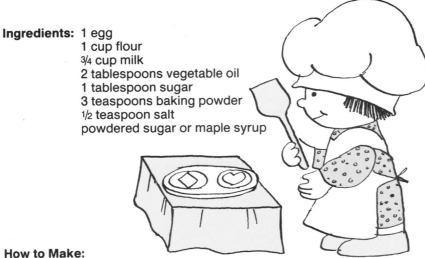

How to Make:

1. In a mixing bowl, beat the egg with a hand beater.

2. Add the flour, milk, vegetable oil, sugar, baking powder, and salt. Beat until smooth.

3. Heat a griddle over medium heat. If you are using an electric griddle, heat to 375°F. Grease the griddle lightly with additional vegetable oil.

4. Using a teaspoon, spoon a small amount of the batter onto the griddle to form simple designs: triangles, arrows, diamonds, hearts, and the like. Space these designs widely apart.

5. When the undersides of the designs have browned slightly, pour about 1/4 cup of batter over each design. Cook until the pancakes are puffy and dry around the edges. Turn with a spatula and cook until the undersides are golden.

6. Remove the pancakes from the griddle and serve them with the designs showing. (The designs will be a darker brown than the rest of the pancakes.)

7. Serve with powdered sugar or maple syrup. (Makes about nine pancakes.)

Ingredients: 1 1/3 cups rice (regular)
2 2/3 cups water
3/4 teaspoon salt
1/3 cup shredded carrot
2 tablespoons melted butter or margarine

How to Make:

1. In a saucepan, heat the rice, water, and salt until the water begins to boil, stirring once or twice.

2. Reduce heat. Cover the pan and simmer for 14 minutes. Do not lift the cover or stir.

3. Remove the pan from heat. Fluff the rice lightly with a fork. Cover the pan and let stand for five to ten minutes.

4. Gently stir in the shredded carrot and melted butter or margarine.

5. Spoon the rice mixture evenly into a greased 4-cup ring mold, pressing the rice down lightly. Then invert a serving plate on the mold. Turn over the plate and mold as a unit. Remove the ring mold. (Makes about 4 cups rice—sixteen 1/4-cup servings.)

Let children help prepare the recipes on this page to feature the meat and meat alternates food group.

PICNIC DRUMSTICKS

Ingredients: ½ cup flour
1 teaspoon salt
1 teaspoon paprika
¼ teaspoon pepper
3 lbs. chicken drumsticks
¼ cup margarine
¼ cup shortening

How to Make:

1. Preheat the oven to 425° F.

2. Measure the flour, salt, paprika, and pepper into a plastic or brown-paper bag.

3. Add two or three drumsticks to the bag and shake until they are well coated. Remove the drumsticks and set aside. Repeat with the remaining drumsticks, always coating only two or three at a time.

4. Place the margarine and shortening in a 13″ × 9″ × 2″ baking pan. Place in the oven just until the margarine and shortening are melted.

5. Place the drumsticks in the pan and bake 30 minutes. Turn them and bake 30 minutes longer. Eat right away or let cool and refrigerate until picnic time. (Makes about 15 drumsticks.)

NUTRITIOUS NUTTY SPREAD

Ingredients: ¼ cup shredded coconut
1 cup peanut butter
¼ cup chopped walnuts
crackers

How to Make:

1. Preheat the oven to 325° F.

2. Spread the shredded coconut on a cookie sheet and place in the oven for about five minutes or until golden brown.

3. Stir the peanut butter, chopped walnuts, and toasted, shredded coconut together in a large bowl.

4. Use the mixture as a spread on crackers. (Makes about 1½ cups.)

Color and cut out the pictures below.
Then cut out the four food-group labels at the bottom of the page.
Paste each label in the blank space at the top of the picture showing
the foods that belong in that food group.
Staple the pictures together to make a minibook.

Name_____

| Milk and Milk Products | Fruits and Vegetables |
| Meat and Meat Alternates | Breads and Cereals |

You need: wheel pattern and grocery-cart
cutouts on this page and page 42
scissors
pencil
oaktag
crayons
empty, clean half-pint milk containers
with the tops cut off
(one for each child)
glue
3″ × 9″ strips of colored construction paper
black construction-paper scraps
discarded magazines with pictures
of food
3″ × 5″ unlined index cards

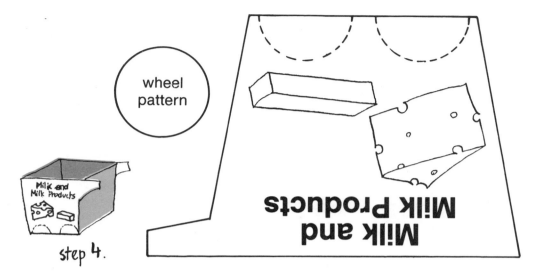

step 4.

Steps:

1. Reproduce the wheel pattern and the four pairs of grocery-cart cutouts on this page and page 42. Make enough so that each child gets one pair of cart cutouts.

2. Ask each child to color his or her pair of cutouts.

3. Next, give each child an empty, clean half-pint milk container with the top cut off. Have each child glue a 3″ × 9″ strip of colored construction paper around the sides of the container.

4. Each child then glues a grocery-cart cutout on opposite sides of the container. See illustration.

5. Cut out the wheel pattern, trace it several times onto oaktag, and then cut out the oaktag patterns.

6. To make wheels for the grocery cart, ask each child to trace an oaktag wheel pattern four times onto black construction paper. Have children cut out the black wheels and glue them in place on their grocery carts, as shown.

7. Distribute magazines with pictures of food to the children. Have each child cut out four small pictures of food belonging to the food group named on his or her grocery cart. Ask children to glue the pictures onto separate 3″ × 5″ unlined index cards. They may then trim the edges of the cards and place them in their grocery carts.

step 6.

Milk and Milk Products

Follow-up Activity:

To make this an individual sorting activity, place a grocery cart representing each of the four food groups on a table. Place the food pictures in a pile next to the carts. In their free time, let individual children place the pictures into the appropriate grocery carts.

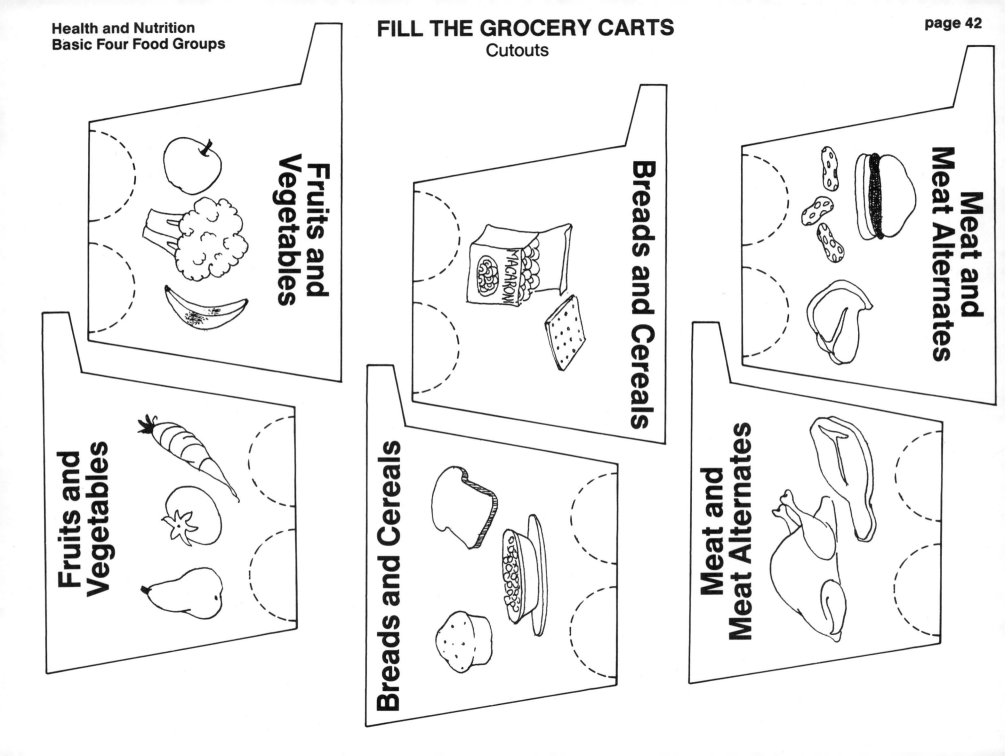

Fruits and Vegetables

Breads and Cereals

Meat and Meat Alternates

Fruits and Vegetables

Breads and Cereals

Meat and Meat Alternates

Name_____

Help Bobby Bear shop for his groceries.
Look at Bobby's list at the left-hand side of the page.
In the picture, find the foods on Bobby's list.

1. Use a green crayon to draw **X**'s on the fruits
   and vegetables that match those on Bobby's list.
2. With a brown crayon, draw **X**'s on the breads
   and cereals that match those on Bobby's list.
3. Draw blue circles around the milk products
   that match those on Bobby's list.
4. Draw red circles around the meat or meat
   alternates that match those on Bobby's list.

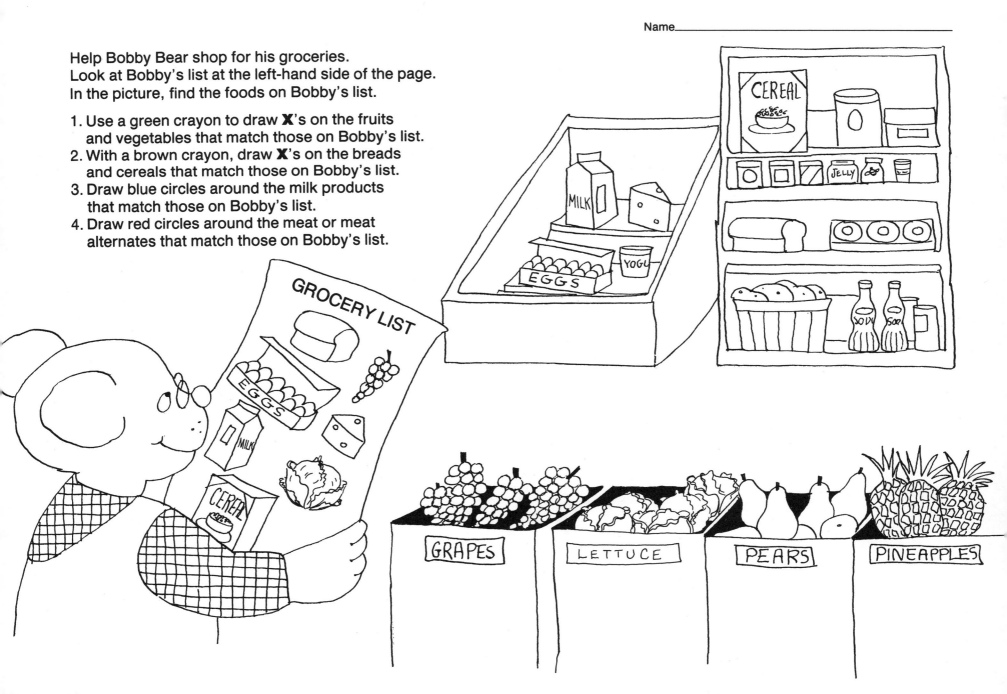

You need: puzzle cutouts on this page
glue
oaktag
scissors

Steps:

1. Make two or three copies of the puzzle cutouts on this page.

2. Glue them onto oaktag and cut them apart along the dotted lines.

3. In their free time, children can put the puzzles together as they review the sources of the different vitamins and minerals.

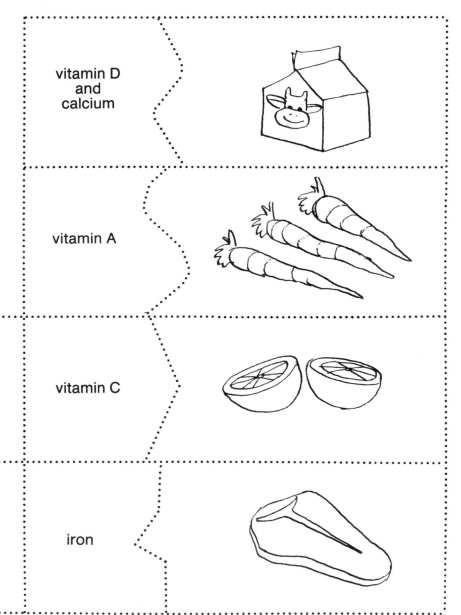

vitamin D
and
calcium

vitamin A

vitamin K

vitamin C

vitamin B

iron

You need: zinnia seeds
several small stones
two large flowerpots with holes
at the bottom for drainage
potting soil
watering can
spoon
plant fertilizer
water
masking tape
marker
plastic cup

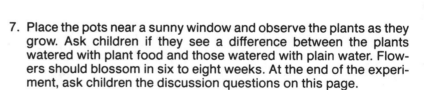

Steps:

1. Discuss with the children how plants, like people, need food to live and grow. Tell children that plant food is different from people food. However, it does the same job of providing nutrients. Mention that soil contains some food for the plants, too.

2. Show the seeds to the children and explain that a seed is the part of a plant from which a new plant will grow.

3. Place several small stones in the bottom of each flowerpot. Then fill the pots with soil and plant the seeds, following the instructions on the package.

4. In the watering can, mix some fertilizer according to the package instructions. Explain that this is plant food and is not good for people.

5. Using masking tape and a marker, label one flowerpot *plant food* and the other *water.* Label the watering can *plant food.*

6. Tell children that the seeds in the flowerpot labeled *plant food* will be watered with the fertilizer from the watering can, and that the seeds in the other flowerpot will be watered only with water. Children may use a plastic cup for the plain water. Let children take turns watering the seeds lightly every two or three days, keeping the soil damp but not soaked.

7. Place the pots near a sunny window and observe the plants as they grow. Ask children if they see a difference between the plants watered with plant food and those watered with plain water. Flowers should blossom in six to eight weeks. At the end of the experiment, ask children the discussion questions on this page.

Discussion Questions:

1. Where does a plant get the food it needs to grow?

2. What kinds of foods do people eat to help them grow?

3. Do things that are not alive, like cars and trucks, need food?

Follow-up Activity:

Have children complete the worksheet on page 46 after doing this experiment.

Look at the pictures in the boxes below.
In each box, circle the picture of the thing that must have food in order to grow.
Then color the pictures you circled.

Name _____

WHAT'S FOR LUNCH?
Easy Recipes

Let children prepare a recipe from this page or page 48 to make their own lunches. You may prefer to do the chopping or cutting and have the children do the stirring, shaking, and arranging.

COLD LUNCHES

DILLY TUNA SANDWICHES

Ingredients: 7-oz. can of tuna, drained
one stalk celery
one dill pickle
¼ cup mayonnaise
margarine
12 slices bread

How to Make:

1. Place the tuna in a bowl and break apart with a fork.

2. Use a knife to chop the celery and the pickle and combine with the tuna. Stir in the mayonnaise with a fork.

3. Spread margarine on the bread slices. Spread the tuna mixture over half of them. Top with the remaining bread slices. (Makes six sandwiches.)

CHEF'S SALAD IN A BAG

Ingredients: one head iceberg lettuce
two tomatoes
eight radishes
six slices cooked ham, turkey, or other meat
six slices American or Swiss cheese
⅓ cup bottled salad dressing

How to Make:

1. Core the lettuce and rinse with cold water. Then tear it into bite-sized pieces and place them on paper towels. Cover and pat with more paper towels to dry.

2. Cut the stem ends from the tomatoes. Cut each tomato into six to eight wedges; cut the wedges in half if you like.

3. Wash and trim the radishes; cut into thin slices.

4. Cut the meat and cheese into strips or bite-sized pieces.

5. Place the lettuce, tomatoes, radishes, meat, and cheese in a plastic bag. Pour in salad dressing. Fasten the bag tightly. Shake the bag a few times to mix all the ingredients. Empty into a salad bowl. (Makes six servings.)

Let children prepare a recipe from this page or page 47 to make their own lunches. You may prefer to do the chopping or cutting and have the children do the stirring, shaking, and arranging.

HOT LUNCHES

PERSONAL PIZZAS

Ingredients: three English muffins
8-oz. can tomato sauce
six slices mozzarella cheese

How to Make:

1. Preheat oven to 325° F. Split English muffins and place on a baking sheet. Place in oven until the tops are just crispy.

2. Spread 1 to 2 tablespoons tomato sauce over each muffin half. (Reserve extra sauce for the next step.) Top with a slice of mozzarella cheese.

3. Using the reserved tomato sauce, have each child make his or her first-name initial on top of the cheese. (Use the tip of the spoon and very little sauce.)

4. Return to the oven and heat about five minutes or until pizzas are hot and cheese has melted. (Makes six personal pizzas.)

SLOPPY JOES

Ingredients: one medium onion, chopped
1 lb. ground beef
10 ¾ oz. can condensed cream of tomato soup
six hamburger buns

How to Make:

1. Preheat oven to 325° F.

2. Place the onion and the beef in a skillet and stir over medium heat until the meat is browned and onions are translucent. Break up the meat as you stir.

3. Carefully drain off the fat.

4. Stir the soup into the meat mixture and simmer over low heat about 15 minutes.

5. Meanwhile, split the buns. Place on a baking sheet and toast in the oven.

6. Serve the meat mixture in the buns. (Makes six sloppy joes.)

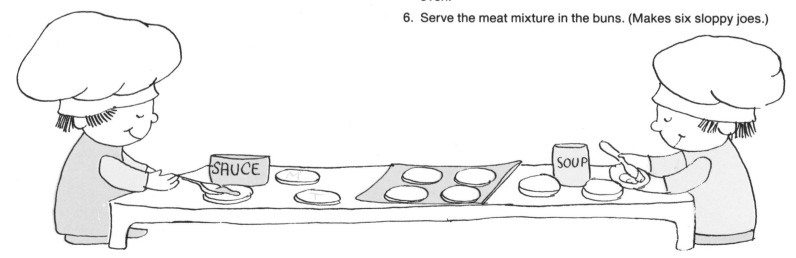

You need: cutouts on page 50
crayons or fine-line markers
glue
oaktag
scissors
two clean, empty 1-qt. milk containers
ruler
two 4″ × 12″ strips of colored construction paper
transparent tape
magazines

Step 5

Steps:

1. Reproduce the cutouts of Healthy Harry and Sweet-Tooth Sue on page 50.

2. With crayons or fine-line markers, color the cutouts. Then glue them onto oaktag.

3. Cut out Healthy Harry and Sweet-Tooth Sue. Then cut out each character's mouth to make an opening.

4. Cut the tops off the two milk containers so that the sides of each container are 4″ high. Wind a 4″ × 12″ strip of colored construction paper around each container and tape in place. Use a crayon or marker to write each character's name on one container.

5. Next, glue the appropriate character onto the labeled sides of the containers, positioning each character so that the mouth opening is higher than the top edge of the container. See illustration.

6. Have children cut out small pictures of foods from discarded magazines. Ask children to cut out pictures of 20 healthy foods and ten snack foods. Glue the pictures onto 2 1/2" squares of oaktag. Let children "feed" these cards to the appropriate character.

7. Place the Healthy Harry and Sweet-Tooth Sue containers on a table. Shuffle the 30 food cards and lay them facedown in a pile next to the containers.

8. In their free time, individual children can go to the table and sort the food cards one by one, inserting the healthy foods through Healthy Harry's mouth and the snack foods through Sweet-Tooth Sue's mouth.

Variation:

Instead of using the food cards, have children cut out small pictures of foods from discarded magazines. Ask children to cut out pictures of healthy foods and snack foods. Glue the pictures onto 2½″ squares of oaktag. Prepare from 25 to 30 cards, and let children "feed" these cards to the appropriate character.

This game reinforces the concept that food is needed for growth, and that some foods are better "growing" foods than others.

You need: food cards created on page 49
growing-child pattern on this page
crayons or markers
scissors
glue
6″ × 9″ oaktag
four envelopes

Steps:

1. Explain that the foods we eat give us energy to play and to grow, and that some foods contain more nutrients than others.

2. Use the food cards created on page 49. Remove four cards from each of the Healthy Food groups and set them aside. Use all ten cards from the Snack Foods group, along with the 24 cards (34 cards in all).

3. Reproduce the growing-child pattern on this page eight times. Color each pattern the same way and cut them out along the solid line perimeters.

4. Make four game boards by gluing four growing-child patterns onto separate pieces of 6″ × 9″ oaktag.

5. Next make four sets of puzzle pieces by cutting the four remaining patterns apart along the dotted lines into four puzzle pieces each (head, upper body, lower body, and legs). Store each set of puzzle pieces in an envelope.

6. Two to four children may play this game. Give each player a game board and an envelope of puzzle pieces. Put the cards facedown in a pile in the center of the players.

7. The youngest child begins by taking the top card. If the card shows a "growing food" (a food from one of the Healthy Food groups), the player takes a puzzle piece from his or her envelope and places it on the appropriate section of the game board. The child to the left of the first player then takes a turn. If a card from the Snack Foods group is picked, the player does nothing and the next child takes a turn.

8. The first player to place all four puzzle pieces on his or her game board wins.

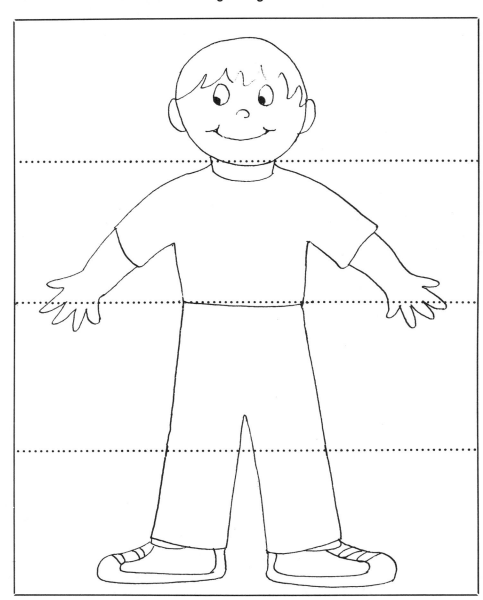

You need: scissors
discarded magazines with pictures of food
glue
colored construction paper
dark marker
thumbtacks or pushpins

Steps:

1. Discuss with children the importance of eating a healthy breakfast every morning. The best breakfasts are those that are made up of one food from each of the basic four food groups. Ask children to tell what they had for breakfast that morning. Have children describe their favorite breakfasts.

2. As evenly as possible, divide the class into four groups. Assign each group one of the basic four food groups.

3. Give each group scissors and discarded magazines with pictures of food. Ask each child to find and cut out a picture of a breakfast food that belongs in his or her assigned food group. Encourage children in each group to find a variety of breakfast foods that fit their assigned category.

4. Have children glue their food pictures onto pieces of colored construction paper.

5. With a dark marker, write the title *Best Breakfasts* on a long strip of construction paper and pin it near the top of a bulletin board.

6. Tell children that they will be arranging their pictures in groups on the bulletin board to create examples of several different healthy breakfasts.

7. Have one child from the milk and milk products group pin his or her picture on the bulletin board. The children in the breads and cereals group then decide which one of their pictured foods would go well with the food from the milk group, and they pin it next to the first picture. Have each of the other groups select a pictured food to pin onto the board to complete the healthy breakfast.

8. Repeat step 7 until most or all of the children's pictures have been used to create examples of healthy breakfasts. Then have children vote on which of the "best breakfasts" they would most enjoy.

You need: function signs on this page and
cutouts on pages 54 and 55
crayons or fine-line markers
glue
9″ × 12″ oaktag
scissors
hole puncher
ruler
yarn
discarded magazines with pictures
of food
large paper clips

Steps:

1. Reproduce the function signs on this page and the letter cutouts on page 54 several times, so that there are both a sign and a letter for each child in your class. Next, make a copy of the vita-man cutout on page 55 for each child.

2. Have children use crayons or fine-line markers to color their vita-men. Ask children to glue their vita-men onto oaktag and then cut them out.

3. Give each child a function sign and the corresponding vitamin letter. Have each child color the letter with a color different from that of his or her vita-man's shirt. Ask children to cut out the letters and glue them on their vita-men.

4. Then have children mount the function signs on oaktag and cut them out.

5. Next punch holes in the vita-men where indicated. Make holes in the corners of each function sign.

6. Attach each child's function sign to his or her vita-man by tying the end of an 8″ piece of yarn through each hole in the upper corners of the function sign, and tying the other end through each hole in the bottom of the vita-man.

7. Using the Major Nutrients in Food reference chart on pages 57 and 58, discuss with children each of the vitamins and how they help us. Name several foods that provide us with these vitamins.

VITAMIN A
HELPS OUR EYES SEE AT NIGHT

VITAMIN B
HELPS US GROW AND KEEPS US HEALTHY

VITAMIN C
HELPS HEAL CUTS AND BUILDS STRONG BLOOD VESSELS

VITAMIN D
HELPS BUILD STRONG BONES AND TEETH

VITAMIN K
HELPS OUR BLOOD TO CLOT

8. Ask each child to look through discarded magazines to find two pictures of foods that contain the vitamin represented by his or her vita-man. Have each child cut out the pictures and glue them onto oaktag. Next, have each child punch a hole in the top of each picture and tie an 8″ piece of yarn through it. The child then ties the other end of the yarn through a hole in a lower corner of the function sign.

9. To make a hanger for each vita-man mobile, bend a large paper clip into an **S** shape. Tie one end of a 12″ piece of yarn onto the paper clip, and the other end through the hole in the top of the vita-man. Suspend the mobiles from the ceiling, and use them to discuss the different vitamins.

A B C D B K

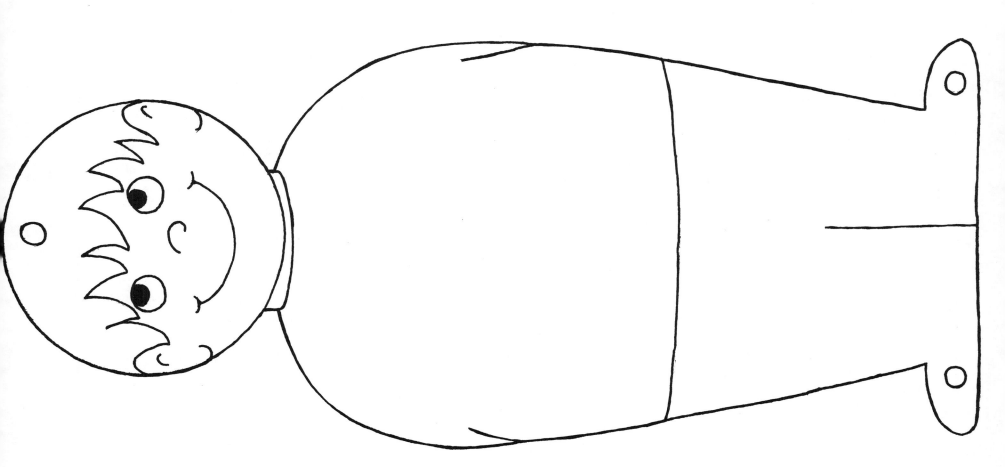

Food Groups	Major Nutrients	Recommended Daily Servings for Children	Examples of One Serving
FATS AND SWEETS		small amounts	one small doughnut one small candy bar
MILK AND MILK PRODUCTS	calcium protein vitamin A vitamin D	2–3 cups of milk and milk products	1 oz. Swiss cheese equals 1 cup milk 1 cup yogurt equals 1 cup milk ½ cup ice cream equals ¼ cup milk
MEAT AND MEAT ALTERNATES	protein iron vitamin B	two or more servings plus one egg	1 oz. meat, fish, or poultry 2 tablespoons peanut butter ½ cup dried beans
FRUITS AND VEGETABLES	vitamin C vitamin A	four or more servings	½ apple or other medium-sized fruit ¼ cup fruit juice ¼ cup cooked vegetables ½ cup berries
BREADS AND CEREALS	carbohydrates iron vitamin B	four or more servings	¼ to ½ cup cooked rice or pasta ½ slice enriched bread ½ cup ready-to-eat cereal

NUTRIENT	WHAT IT DOES	SOURCES
protein	builds body tissues	meats, fish, and poultry; eggs; dried beans; nuts; milk; cheese
carbohydrates (starches and sugars)	provide energy	complex carbohydrates: fruits; vegetables such as corn, beets, potatoes; rice; pasta simple carbohydrates: sugar, honey, candy, cakes, sweets
fats	provide energy; transport fat-soluble vitamins (A, D, K)	oils; butter and margarine; fatty meats; cream; egg yolks; whole milk saturated: animal fats unsaturated: plant fats (generally)
water	aids digestion, excretion; regulates body temperature	water, teas, juices, soups, fruits, vegetables

MAJOR NUTRIENTS IN FOOD
Teacher Reference Chart

NUTRIENT	WHAT IT DOES	SOURCES
vitamins water soluble: C (ascorbic acid)	promotes healing; keeps tissues (especially gums and blood vessels) healthy	citrus fruits and juices, tomatoes, broccoli, strawberries
B complex	necessary for growth, general health, normal digestion	meats, fish, poultry, milk, eggs, whole grains, leafy green vegetables
fat soluble: A	keeps skin and lining of digestive and respiratory systems healthy; helps night vision	liver, carrots, yams, squash, leafy green vegetables, melons, broccoli, milk, egg yolk
D	aids bone and tooth development by enhancing calcium utilization	liver, milk enriched with vitamin D, fatty fish
K	promotes blood clotting	dark green leafy vegetables, liver, tomatoes
minerals calcium	necessary for bone and tooth development	milk and milk products, collards, kale, turnip greens, sardines, and canned salmon
iron	carries oxygen in blood, builds red blood cells	liver, lean red meat, poultry, dried beans, egg yolk, beet greens, spinach

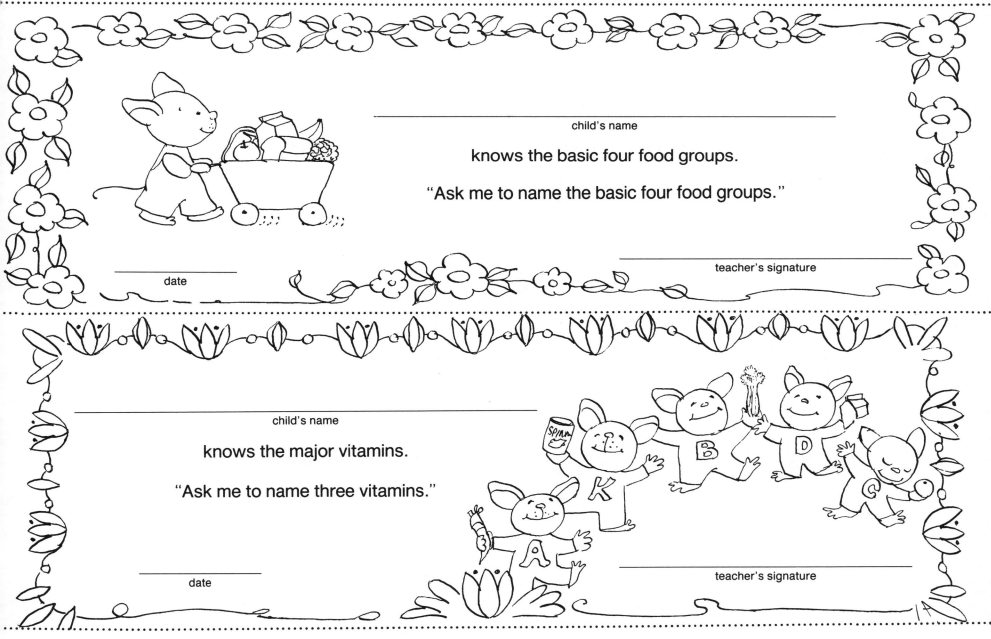

knows the basic four food groups.

"Ask me to name the basic four food groups."

child's name

date

teacher's signature

child's name

knows the major vitamins.

"Ask me to name three vitamins."

date

teacher's signature

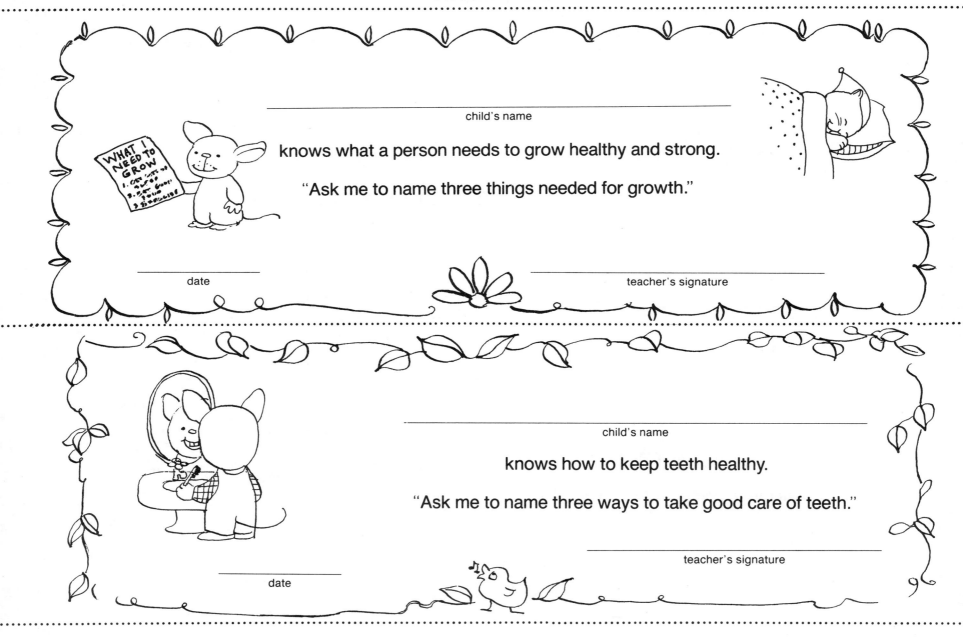

_____
child's name

knows what a person needs to grow healthy and strong.

"Ask me to name three things needed for growth."

_____
date

_____
teacher's signature

_____
child's name

knows how to keep teeth healthy.

"Ask me to name three ways to take good care of teeth."

_____
teacher's signature

_____
date

You need: labels, stickers, and cutout pieces of boxes from different foods (canned fruit labels, banana stickers, raisin boxes, and so on)
9″ × 12″ colored construction paper
glue
scissors

Optional: clear plastic adhesive

Steps:

1. Ask children to bring in labels, stickers, and cutout pieces of boxes from their favorite foods.

2. Have children select a few labels, stickers, and cutout pieces of boxes from each of the food groups.

3. Give each child a 9″ × 12″ piece of colored construction paper. Ask him or her to arrange the food labels, stickers, and box parts in a collage on the paper. Explain to children that they can overlap parts of the labels.

4. Have children glue the food labels, stickers, and box parts onto their papers.

5. After the glue has dried, laminate the collages or cover both sides with clear plastic adhesive. Trim the edges evenly.

6. Let children use their food place mats at snack time. Be sure to wipe the place mats clean after each use. The place mats can be used to initiate a discussion of the basic four food groups and food preferences.

Variation:

Children can make their place mats using pictures of foods from magazines, or they may cut food shapes from different colored construction paper. (For example, children could cut apple shapes from red paper, banana shapes from yellow paper, or lettuce from green paper.) Then have children follow the steps above to complete their place mats.

FOOD MATHEMATICS
Addition and Subtraction Worksheet

Add or subtract the healthy foods shown in each problem.
Then, to the right of each problem, circle the correct answer.

Name _____

Have children make these molded food paperweights to give as presents to their parents.

You need: waxed paper
4 cups flour
1 cup salt
1½ cups water
toothpicks
craft sticks
tempera paints
paintbrushes

Optional: polyurethane spray

Steps:

1. Give each child some waxed paper to place on his or her work surface.

2. Make the clay by mixing the flour, salt, and water in a large bowl. (You will need to use your hands to mix thoroughly.)

3. Divide the dough among the children so that each child has a generous handful. Have the children knead the dough until it is pliable, about five minutes.

4. Have each child mold the dough into a food shape: an apple, carrot, asparagus stalk, doughnut, roll, ice-cream cone, and the like. (Or you can ask the children to divide the dough into four portions and make one small item from each of the four food groups.)

5. Have the children define the features of their foods with the tip of a craft stick or with the blunt end of a toothpick. For example, use the blunt end of a toothpick to add texture to a clay strawberry; indicate the peel on a banana or the layers of a piece of cake with a craft stick. Small pieces of dough can also be added to create special features (for example, individual peas in a pea pod, the hull on a strawberry). But always put a dab of water on the spot where the piece will be added—baking will "cement" it in place.

6. Place the dough shapes on a cookie sheet and bake at 250°F for about two hours.

7. Have the children paint the foods.

8. After the paint is dry, the foods may be sprayed with polyurethane. (Note: Do not allow the children to use the spray.) Makes about thirty 3″ shapes.

Note: Because this dough dries out very quickly, keep any unused dough covered with a damp cloth or in a sealed container. Slow workers may have to dampen the dough with water from time to time.

Variations:

1. To make magnets for a refrigerator or cupboard door, follow the directions above, except have the children flatten one side of their dough foods. After the shapes have been baked and the paint is dry, glue a magnet onto the flat side of each piece.

2. Before baking, make a hole near the top of the shape with the blunt end of a toothpick or a plastic straw. Yarn or string can then be looped through the hole to make a hanging kitchen ornament.

3. Ask the children to bring in clean lidded jars from home. Have the children paint the lids and glue on their food shapes. The jars can be used for refrigerator or shelf storage at home.

Use these games to help children learn to recognize different types of food and to distinguish nutritious foods from less nutritious foods.

You need: food cards you create (see below)
glue
oaktag
scissors

Optional: clear plastic adhesive

To Prepare the Game:

1. Create a set of food cards that show examples from each of the basic food groups, as well as snack foods that are low in nutritional value. Cut index cards in half to use as the food cards, then draw one food on each.

2. Create ten different cards for each food group and the snack group. For example: *dairy:* milk, types of cheeses, butter, yogurt, ice cream; *meat:* fish, steak, turkey, ham, sausages, chicken; *fruits and vegetables:* banana, orange, lettuce, corn; *breads and cereals:* pasta, slice of bread, oatmeal, crackers, rice; *snacks:* candy, doughnut, lollipop.

3. Cover the cards with clear plastic adhesive to make them more sturdy.

How to Play:

For younger children: (Two to four children may play.)

1. Use 20 of the food cards, selecting four from each of the five food groups.

2. Have one player lay the cards facedown on the floor or on a table in four rows of five cards each.

3. Let the youngest child begin. Each player tries to find pairs of food cards from the same food group. The first player turns over any two cards for all to see. If the foods shown on the cards belong to the same food group, the player keeps them, and the

child to his or her left takes a turn. If the cards are not from the same food group, the player turns them facedown again, and the child to the left of the first player takes a turn. Children should try to remember which foods were pictured on any card turned facedown again.

4. The players take turns until all the cards have been paired. The player who collects the greaest number of pairs is the winner.

For older children: (Two to four children may play.)

1. Have one child deal out five cards to each player. The players hold their cards without showing them to the other players.

2. Place the rest of the cards facedown in a pile in the center of the players.

3. The youngest child goes first. Each player tries to collect one card from each of the five food groups. The first player takes the top card from the pile and decides if he or she needs that card. If the player needs the card, he or she keeps it and discards another card from his or her hand, placing it faceup next to the pile of cards. If the player does not need that card, he or she discards it faceup next to the pile.

4. The player to the left of the first player then takes a turn. If he or she needs the discarded card, the player takes it and discards another card from his or her hand. If the player does not need the discarded card, he or she takes the top card from the pile and keeps it or discards it. Players must keep five cards in their hands at all times. During a turn, a player may take the top card from either the pile or the discard pile, but may not take a card from underneath the top cards.

5. The game continues clockwise until one player has collected one card from each of the five groups. He or she then lays the five cards faceup in front of him or her and calls out "Five food fancy!" and becomes the winner.